W9-BIU-159

For two thousand years, writers and artists have fastened stories to each of Cleopatra's features: descriptions of her eyes, mouth, nose and hair have become accounts of her compelling personality; explanations of her fascination, morality tales, poems. This anthology follows her face to trace the secrets of her soul.

Imagine a woman of sufficient interest to throw future ages into a labyrinth of dreams ... with the mind and a body to captivate a cæsar, a world-conqueror ... Did such a person exist, or was she only a figment of the imagination?

Michael Foss

We possess no authentic portrait of Cleopatra, and the features of the Queen have left not the slightest reflection on this vast earth, where she caused so much mourning and misfortune.

Anatole France

The gigantic figures graven on the crumbling walls of the temple at Denderah do not enable us to distinguish her ... the woman who was all intelligence, love, audacity, flame, and tempest.

Claude Ferval

It is as if the darkness closes around her.

Enzo Gualazzi

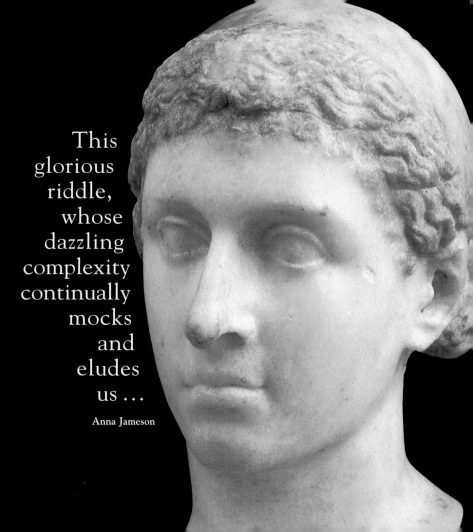

This glorious riddle, whose dazzling complexity continually mocks and eludes us ...

Anna Jameson

Her beauty was such that men boasted of it in the most distant lands of the Roman Empire. The poets and historians of the day, Greek as well as Roman, sang of Cleopatra as of a living Venus, a second Helen, the Aphrodite of the Nile ... this princess must undoubtedly have been extraordinarily beautiful, for, after two thousand years, her beauty still lights up the page of the historian.

Désiré de Bernáth

"She beggars description."

Henry Brooke

Cleopatra, in splendour of love's imaginings, holds earth and its sun, heaven and all eternities in her gaze.

George Wilson Knight

She is the living poetry
of a world devoid of any principles …
a spirit without conscience of duty
and an unbridled passion …

Henri Blaze de Bury

**Cleopatra has in her heart the flame
which purifies all: she loves.**

François-Victor Hugo

**Oh God, how happy would he be who could
hold that lady naked and willing in his arms!**

Jean de Tuim

She cannot be explained,
she can only be felt.

Sir Laurence Olivier

Before
the thought
of Cleopatra
every man is
an Antony.

Arthur Symons

Cleopatra is a woman in the most lovely and the most cursed sense.

Heinrich Heine

"Her thought is a world, and her heart is an abyss."

Delphine de Girardin

There is in her a streak of mysterious and obscene evil.

George Wilson Knight

Shall she not have the hearts of us
To shatter, and the loves therein
To shred between her fingers thus?

Algernon Charles Swinburne

Designed by Michelle Lovric and Lisa Pentreath.
Text and compilation © 2001 Michelle Lovric,
Covent Garden, London
Manufactured in China by Imago

Published by British Museum Press
A division of The British Museum Company Ltd,
46 Bloomsbury Street, London WC1B 3QQ
ISBN 0-7141-1937-7
First published 2001

A catalogue record for this book is available from the British Library.

CLEOPATRA'S
FACE
fatal beauty

Michelle Lovric

THE BRITISH MUSEUM PRESS

CONTENTS

Woman of women, quintessentiated Eve,

"She deserves More worlds than I can lose."

John Dryden

or rather Eve and the serpent in one...

Georg Brandes

Cleopatra has left us no written word. We can read her only in the spectacle she created of and for herself. Cleopatra identified herself with Isis, the great goddess of Egypt: part mother, part lover. We can also read Cleopatra's ambitions and tastes in the two men she chose to love: the Masters of the known world, the Roman Empire.

We have come to see sexuality as empowering. Cleopatra was ahead of us. Cleopatra seduced with food, gold, peacocks and pearls. Both Julius Cæsar and Antony were wooed with stupendous banquets: such delicious creativity being a clear metaphor for sexual invitation. In Cleopatra's case, the reason was also more practical: her spectacles were displays of her wealth and power, to win recognition of herself, and her nation, as major players on the world stage. Most of all though, of course, Cleopatra seduced with herself.

Despite her universal fame, not one single contemporary description of Cleopatra's face, by an eyewitness, has survived. Plutarch, writing two centuries after her death, had access to several such accounts, which are now unfortunately lost. For the rest, historians, playwrights, and poets have had to rely on their imaginations … and the accounts of Octavian's propagandists.

What we think we know of Cleopatra has been coloured, indelibly, by the Romans. Cleopatra was a useful tool in their internal campaigns: a non-Roman enemy for soldiers weary of killing fellow Romans to further the ambitions of the rival Roman leaders. Cleopatra could, conveniently, symbolize everything their noble, democratic, straightforward race had to fear. She was an absolute despot: a genre Republican Rome found politically incorrect. She was also a foreigner – with all the consequent connotations of depravity, dishonesty, opulence and cruelty. And she was a woman – capriciousness, weakness and irrationality incarnate.

Worse, the Romans saw Cleopatra as an unnatural Woman, who violated accepted feminine codes to choose her own sexual partners, exercising both political and

CLEOPATRA WAS AN EGYPTIAN WOMAN WHO BECAME

erotic power over them. She turned tough Roman generals into love-slaves, luring them into the self-indulgent, emasculating delights of her bed and her dining room. The fact that she married two of her brothers, and had her sister, Arsinoe, killed, had far less shock value: such events did not threaten Rome, or Rome's image of itself.

Even when the Roman Empire dissolved, it took centuries for a new image of Cleopatra to emerge, so dominating was the view of the Roman writers. But as the world reshaped itself, so was the image of Cleopatra refashioned to a useful parable for the spirit of the times again and again. Writers of the pre-Shakespearean period tended to see nobility in her suicide: the redemptive act of dying for love was honoured by the tradition of courtly love. In the plays and poems of this period, Cleopatra admits her wrong-doings before she dies, and thereby renders Antony innocent, as Adam is excused complicity in Original Sin, by the fact that it was Eve who handed him the apple. Elizabethan writers saw Cleopatra's and Antony's suicides as a morality tale about passion and fidelity. Shakespeare used the story to show the danger of excessive love. The 17th- and 18th-century writers turned their attentions to the private struggle of a weak, passionate woman, caught up in a political whirlwind beyond her ken. Others pointed to her as the embodiment of feminine manipulation and commercial harlotry.

The Romantics thrilled to the Cleopatran scenario of passion-in-death. In the Victorian period, Cleopatra expressed a masochistic fantasy of murderous sexual rapaciousness. By the end of the 19th century, Cleopatra had started to camp it up. In the 20th century, she was admired as the ultimate "it" girl, behaving badly, but doing it in style. A century which saw its dreams played out on the silver screen took Cleopatra as one of its most dominant icons. The most glamorous and wayward actresses of every generation have taken her role, sometimes in their private lives as well.

The 21st century will bring a new interpretation again to Cleopatra, for whatever we want, in the way of a surpassing female icon, Cleopatra will be it. Her eyes, nose, lips will be painted on our consciousness as long as there is passion, beauty and death.

Sculpture of Cleopatra, Rosicrucian Egyptian Museum.

69 BC Cleopatra VII born, the third child of Ptolemy Auletes ("the flute-player").

58 BC Ptolemy Auletes is obliged to seek Rome's protection for his crumbling regime.

51 BC Ptolemy Auletes dies. Cleopatra, aged eighteen, and her brother, Ptolemy XIII, aged ten, are joint heirs.

49 BC Cleopatra is driven out of Alexandria by her brother and his supporters.

48 BC Civil War in Italy. Julius Cæsar arrives in Egypt, in pursuit of his rival, Pompey. The Egyptians murder Pompey. Cæsar and Cleopatra become lovers. Ptolemy XIII drowns in the Nile. Cæsar restores Cleopatra to the throne with her brother Ptolemy XIV. The siblings marry.

46 BC Cæsar returns to Rome. Cleopatra follows him. She probably meets Antony there for the first time.

44 BC Cæsar is murdered. Cleopatra, who has borne him a son, Cæsarion, returns to Alexandria. Ptolemy XIV is murdered. Cæsarion is made joint ruler of Egypt with his mother. Civil war in Italy. A new triumvirate – Antony, Octavian (Cæsar's heir) and Lepidus – defeat Cæsar's assassins. Rivalry arises between Octavian and Antony, who decides to raise money in Egypt.

41 BC Cleopatra and Antony meet at Tarsus, and become lovers. He returns with her to Alexandria, where they live in splendour. Cleopatra bears him twins, Alexander Helios and Cleopatra Selene.

40 BC Antony returns to Rome after the death of his wife, Fulvia. To seal a peace treaty with Octavian, Antony marries his sister, Octavia, who bears him two children, but hostility grows between the two men.

37 BC Antony returns to Alexandria and grants Cleopatra extensive territories in the Middle East. Cleopatra builds a fleet and provisions Antony's army.

36 BC Antony departs for a war against the Parthians. Cleopatra bears him a third child, Ptolemy Philadelphus.

34 BC In a ceremony, known as The Donations of Alexandria, Antony proclaims Cleopatra and her children kings and queens and grants them further large realms. He recognizes Cæsarion as the legal heir of Julius Cæsar – defying Octavian, who declares war on Cleopatra.

32 BC Antony and Cleopatra start assembling their fleet for the final encounter with Octavian. Antony divorces Octavia. Octavian declares war on Cleopatra.

31 BC September 2nd, the Battle of Actium. Cleopatra flees, followed by Antony.

30 BC Octavian invades Egypt. Antony, believing that Cleopatra has killed herself, falls on his sword. He is taken to the Treasure House in which she has locked herself, and dies in her arms. After hearing that Octavian plans to exhibit her in chains in his triumph in Rome, Cleopatra kills herself by applying an asp to her breast.

Note: Many writers refer to Octavian as Cæsar. Antony's and Charmian's names are also subject to variations. To avoid confusion, the names of Antony, Cæsar, Charmian and Octavian are standardized throughout the book. For reasons of space, the full attribution is given only the first time an author or work appears in the book.

French illuminated manuscript, 15th century,
Deaths of Antony and Cleopatra, © The British Museum.

Cleopatra and her story have the weight
of originary myth in Western culture.

Mary Hamer, contemporary English writer,
from *Signs of Cleopatra, History, Politics, Representation*, 1993.

CLEOPATRA'S

The grandmother of Cleopatra was a concubine; her mother is not known for certain. Given all the uncertainties of her ancestry, one scholar has estimated her blood as 32 parts Greek, 27 parts Macedonian and 5 parts Persian. It is a reasonable guess. If she was black, no one mentioned it.

Michael Foss (b. 1937), British writer, from *The Search for Cleopatra*, 1987.

Greek of the Greeks, her quick blood spoke in every delicate, swift gesture, in light lures and laughters ... she had the Greek ardour and courage of her royal line, and wore them with a defiant grace and humour, quick flashes of temper and lovely relentings, teasing, sparkling, swift to love or hate ...

E. Barrington [Eliza Louisa Moresby Beck],
early 20th-century Canadian writer, from *The Laughing Queen*, 1929.

Brought up in the arts and manners of Hellas, she possessed the grace, the eloquence, the elegant familiarity, the ingenious audacity of her race. Neither the gods of Egypt nor the monsters of Africa ever gained a hold upon her laughing soul.

Anatole France [Jacques-Anatole-François Thibault] (1844–1924), French writer,
from the preface to Théophile Gautier's *Cleopatra*, 1899 edition.

BLOOD

Cleopatra's tawniness contributes to the sense of her ancient and mysterious sexuality ...

Janet Adelman (b. 1941), American writer,
from *The Common Liar*, an essay on *Antony and Cleopatra*, 1973.

Aphrodite breathes this hue on the faces and figures of her favourites only ...

Georg Moritz Ebers (1837–98), German Egyptologist,
novelist and poet, from *Cleopatra, a Romance*, 1894.

"No blood was in her veins, but the sun's blood.
Sweet Hathor lived in her eyes and her dimpled knees."

Words spoken by Cæsar
Vachel Lindsay (1879–1931), American poet, from "The Trial of the
Dead Cleopatra in her Beautiful and Wonderful Tomb", 1923.

"Even through her frailties, one senses her royal blood,
One trembles, one is conquered, but so voluptuously!"

Diomedes, Act I, 1 from Delphine de Girardin's *Cléopâtre*, 1847.
Rachel Félix, the celebrated French actress, performed in Madame de
Girardin's play for the first time on November 13th that year.

19

Sculpture of Cleopatra, Hermitage Museum.

But beware, beloved, Ptolemy women engender violence,
Command money, men, and manumission.
Cleopatra revels in infanticide, regicide, and patricide.
Ptolemy the builder of the museum fathered
Ptolemy II, who exiled his wife to marry his sister.
Ptolemy IV murdered his father, brother, and mother;
Married his sister but murdered her.
Ptolemy V married Cleopatra and fathered
Ptolemy VI, who married his sister Cleopatra, who
Married both her two brothers, of which one brother,
Ptolemy VIII, murdered his child by Cleopatra out of
Vengeance on this wife and sister when she became queen.
He then married his wife Cleopatra's daughter by her
Second husband, his brother and she, his niece.
Ptolemy VII, murdered by his father and uncle, who had
Married his mother, who was also his sister, whom he

history to her lover

Murdered on her wedding night, was also brother to
Ptolemy IX, the other son murdered by his father,
Or his aunt, or his half sister.
Ptolemy X married his sister Cleopatra, but
Ptolemy XI murdered his mother Cleopatra.
Ptolemy XII married his cousin Cleopatra but murdered
Her and was himself murdered by the people.
Ptolemy X, a son of Ptolemy XII, fathered a
Cleopatra whom he murdered to regain the throne,
Leaving this Cleopatra beside you and her two brothers,
Ptolemy XIV, who drowned fleeing a lost battle, and
Ptolemy XV, whom I, Cleopatra, married and murdered.

Barbara Chase-Riboud (b. 1949), American poet, writer and sculptor,
from *Portrait of a Nude Woman as Cleopatra*, 1987.
This cycle of poems was inspired by Rembrandt's drawing of the same name.

21

"My great-grandmother's great-grandmother was a black kitten of the sacred white cat; and the river Nile made her his seventh wife. That is why my hair is so wavy. And I always want to be let do as I like, no matter whether it is the will of the gods or not: that is because my blood is made with Nile water."

Cleopatra to Cæsar
from George Bernard Shaw's play, *Cæsar and Cleopatra*, 1889.
It was produced in Berlin and New York in 1906 and in London in 1907.
The film version was first shown in London in 1945.

This capricious, pleasure-loving, fickle, feverish coquette, this ancient *parisienne*, this goddess of life flutters and rules over Egypt, the silent petrified land of the dead.

Heinrich Heine (1797–1856), German poet and critic,
from "Shakespeare's Mädchen und Frauen" (Shakespeare's Women and Girls) in *Sämtliche Schriften*, 1838.

Was not Cleopatra

Vivien Leigh and Claude Rains in Cæsar and Cleopatra, 1945.

h e r s e l f   a   s p h i n x ?

Gaston Delayen, 20th-century French historical writer, from *Cleopatra*, 1934.

CLEOPATRA'S
EYES

Under those low large lids of hers
She hath the histories of all time.

Algernon Charles Swinburne (1837–1909), English poet,
from *Cleopatra*, 1866.

Will I call you a mortal woman, or an immortal goddess,
if in one flick of your eye, you make yourself mistress
of the master of the masters of the world?

Paganino Gaudenzio (1596–1649), Italian controversialist,
from *Di Cleopatra Reina D'Egitto: la Vita Considerata*, 1642.

Head of a Queen, Brooklyn Museum of Art.

Her eyes were shaded by narrow eyelids, and eyebrows slightly arched and delicately outlined. We cannot attempt by description to convey an idea of their brilliancy: it was a fire, a languor, a sparkling limpidity which might have made even the dog-headed Anubis giddy; every glance of her eyes was in itself a poem.

Théophile Gautier (1811–72), French poet and author,
from *Cleopatra*, 1845.

Her Eyes darted Beams more Glorious than the richest Diamond could sparkle.

Gautier de Costes de La Calprenède (1610–63), French dramatist and writer,
from *Cleopatra*, 1658.

Her eyes, brimming with sweetness, bore an indefinable expression which seemed to attract and defy at the same time.

Jeanne Cantel, early 20th-century French novelist,
from *La Reine Cléopâtra*, with a preface by Anatole France, 1914.

"Her look is as deep as an ocean-wave."

Harmaki, Cleopatra's would-be lover, Act II, 1
from Arne Christiansen's play, *Cleopatra*, 1893.
The storyline is based on Rider Haggard's tale.

"Her eyes have pow'r
beyond Thessalian charms
To draw the moon from heaven."

Ventidius to Octavia, Act IV
from John Dryden's play, *All For Love*, 1677.

Dryden's play ruled the stage from its inception, surpassing Shakespeare's in popularity for nearly a century. The first production of Dryden's play featured Mrs Boutell as Cleopatra, and was seen in 1678. It was the author's favourite work. He declared that he wrote it to please himself. Elizabeth Barry and Mrs Oldfield, Mrs Bellamy, Peg Woffington, Mrs Hartley, Miss Younge, the famous actresses of their days, also took the central role. Anna Jameson, writing in 1832, observed that his Cleopatra is "a mere common-place 'All for love' heroine, full of constancy and fine sentiments".

"She is all heav'nly: never any man
But seeing her was ravished with her sight.
The Alabaster covering of her face,
The coral colour her two lips engraines,
Her beaming eyes, two Suns of this our world …"

Diomedes, Act I
from Robert Garnier's play, *Marc Antoine*, 1578.

Garnier's depiction of Cleopatra's lover has much in common with Shakespeare's. Cleopatra blames herself for the downfall of the noble man, but the playwright's sympathy is clearly with her own sufferings.

Note: Dio Cassius records that Octavian was so afraid of the power of her magnificent eyes that he kept his own fixed on the floor in their only interview, lest he, too, succumb to her witchery.

... As if the very eyes of love
Shone through her shutting lids, and stole
The slow looks of a snake or dove;
As if her lips absorbed the whole
Of love, her soul the soul thereof ...

Algernon Charles Swinburne, from *Cleopatra*, 1866.

"Downe from her eyes distils a Christall tyde,
Which at his comming she would dry againe,
And sodainly would turne her head a side
As though unwilling to reveale her paine.
Thus in his presence ravished with joy,
She smiles, and shewes, what mirth she can devize:
But in his absence drowned with annoy
She seemes to take her life from those his eyes."

Plancus describes how Cleopatra has seduced Antony, Act III, 2
from Samuel Brandon's play, *The Tragicomoedi of the vertuous Octavia*, 1598.
The play is closely modelled on Samuel Daniel's Cleopatra, and its historical
content draws from Thomas North's Plutarch.

Her eyes were like two rays of the great moon,
When Mediterranean storms destroy the ships.
She looked at him. And the eyes of Antony
Became the idiot eye-holes of a helmet,
The visor down. And his world-flashing sword
Was smoke and dust – his face a wavering flame.

Vachel Lindsay, from "The Trial of the Dead Cleopatra in her Beautiful and
Wonderful Tomb", 1923.

"A stealing Shower of Tears roll'd down her Cheeks,
Like Dew-drops trickling o'er the Bloom of Roses."

Photinus describing Cleopatra's first attempt to win Antony's pity, Act II
from Colley Cibber's play, *Cæsar in Ægypt*, 1725.

28

Cléopâtre, "L'Encaustique sur ardoise", The British Library.

"... my own too roving eye
Was drawn astray into the eyes
of that Cleopatra!"

Antony's ghost, Act I, 1
from Étienne Jodelle's play, *Cléopâtre Captive*, 1553.
Jodelle wrote his play when he was 20, and he
played the tragic Queen himself in its first
performance. Jodelle's play is an innovation in
that it commences after the death of Antony and
concerns only the last day of Cleopatra's life.
However, Antony's vengeful shade makes an
appearance, calling Cleopatra to come to him
beyond the grave, to which she had led him.
Cleopatra truly repents of her sins, and her suicide
is an act of purification.

"O! I have drank my Ruin,
at my Eyes!"

Antony to Cæsar, Act III
from Colley Cibber's play, *Cæsar in Ægypt*, 1725.

"Thy kisses more than paid me for the pain
That I forget. The Empire is well lost –
I have reigned o'er thy soul.
    All else is naught
When thy sweet eyes look love."

The dying Antony forgives Cleopatra
for her betrayals, Act IV from
Louis Payen's [Albert Liénard] libretto for the
opera, *Cleopatra*, by Jules Massenet, 1915.

CLEOPATRA'S NOSE

Silver coin showing Cleopatra,
© The British Museum.

Had
Cleopatra's
nose
been
shorter,
the face
of the
world
would
have
changed.

Blaise Pascal (1623–62),
French mathematician and
religious philosopher,
from *Pensées*, 1670.

Everything that poetry can do, is done, to make us forget the faults of Cleopatra, and to incline us to think that a world was well lost for that *petit nez retroussé*.

William Maginn (1793–1842), Irish writer, from *Shakespeare Papers*, 1838/9.

If the nose had not been so long and pointed, the wayward and ardently voluptuous woman shown in this profile might pass for beautiful.

Henry Houssaye (1848–1911), French historian, from *Cleopatra, A Study*.

32

There exist medals of Cleopatra ... All represent her with large, harsh features, and an exceedingly long nose ... if we are to believe the medals, this nose was out of all proportion; but we will not believe them; no, not if people should put before us all the collections of medals in the Bibliothèque Nationale, the British Museum, and the Cabinet of Vienna ... The features which caused Cæsar to forget the empire of the world were not spoilt by a ridiculous nose.

Anatole France, from the preface to Théophile Gautier's *Cleopatra*, 1899 edition.

All that we can feel certain about is that she had not a short nose.

Philip W. Sergeant, early 20th-century English writer,
from *Cleopatra of Egypt – Antiquity's Queen of Romance*, 1909.

Constance Collier as Cleopatra, 1906.

But alas, that nose!

Lord Berners (Gerald Tyrwhitt-Wilson) (1883–1950), English writer,
from *The Romance of a Nose*, 1941.

In Lord Berners' novel, Cleopatra is the most beautiful and intellectually active woman in the world, but her nose is a monstrous disfigurement. Aided by Apollodorus, she undergoes plastic surgery. The surgeon parades 30 slave-girls in front of her so that she may select a new nose, but she orders him to copy a stone bust of a Syrian woman which she has brought with her. The woman has a face identical to Cleopatra's apart from the nose (and is now, according to the novel, to be found at the British Museum – see opposite page). When Cleopatra sees her beautiful new nose for the first time she throws off all her clothes and performs cartwheels.

33

In all the representations of her she wears a smile, which was no doubt characteristic; so consummate a mistress of the art of fascination knew well the power of a winning smile.

Villiers Stuart (1827–95), English writer, from *Nile Gleanings*, 1879.

Her mouth is fragrant as a vine,
A vine with birds in all its boughs.

Algernon Charles Swinburne, from *Cleopatra*, 1866.

CLEOPATRA'S M

OUTH

Salvatore Fiume, Cleopatra,

It was

impossible

to converse

with her,

without

being

immediately

captivated

by her.

Dio Cassius
(c. AD 150–235),
Roman politician
and historian, from
Roman History.
He explains that
this, as much as
her beauty, led
to Julius Cæsar
falling deeply in
love with her.

In conversation, Cleopatra was gentle, pleasant, graceful, and, knew how, in the most exquisite and intelligent manner, to make men of any kind or class feel comfortable; the wisdom of her words was as great as her readiness to respond to them; her words were accompanied by the most graceful of gestures; her movements were melting and yet well- considered; her voice was soft, sweet and suave …

Giulio Landi (1500–80), Italian writer,
from *La Vita de Cleopatra Regina d'Egitto*, 1551.
In this emotional play, Landi praises Cleopatra's powers of leadership and intelligence. Landi drew his story from Plutarch and his own imagination. He is sympathetic towards Cleopatra.

She could easily turn her tongue, like a many-stringed instrument, to any language she pleased.

Plutarch (before AD 50–after AD 120), Greek biographer, from *Parallel Lives.*

Her warbling voice, a lyre of widest range
Struck by all passion, did fall down and glance
From tone to tone, and glided thro' all change
Of liveliest utterance.

Alfred, Lord Tennyson (1809–92), English poet, from "A Dream of Fair Women".

36

She possessed the gift of discussing trifles intellectually, combining seductive femininity with spiritual charm.

Oskar von Wertheimer, early 20th-century German writer, from *Cleopatra, A Royal Voluptuary*, 1931.

… though there were some women in Rome that were her equals in beauty, none could rival her in the charms of seducing conversation.

William Pinch, 19th-century English writer, from *The Sufferings of Royalty*, 1855.

This is why Mark Antony loved Cleopatra so much and preferred her to his wife Octavia, who was a hundred times more agreeable and beautiful than Cleopatra; but Cleopatra had such a touching way of talking and little turns of phrase so in keeping with her lascivious charms and graces, that Mark Antony forsook all for her love.

Pierre de Bourdeille, Seigneur de Brantôme (1540?–1614), French historian and biographer, from *Les Vies des Dames Galantes*, 1666.

She spoke the loveliest Latin. Her voice slipped along the vowels like cream.

E. Barrington, from *The Laughing Queen*, 1929.

Sculpture, possibly of Cleopatra, The Vatican Museum.

"... for eloquence,
The sea-green Sirens taught
    her voice their flatt'ry;
And, while she speaks,
    night steals upon the day,
Unmarked of those that hear."

Ventidius to Octavia, Act IV
from John Dryden's play, *All For Love*, 1677.

"But tis hir Syren tongue that dooth delight,
Her craftie Cyrces wit which hath him caught ...
Then Meeremaid-like his scences she invades,
With sweetest nectar of a sugered tongue:
Unto her will, she ever him persuades,
The force of her words witch-craft is so strong."

Plancus describes how Cleopatra has seduced Antony, Act III, 2
from Samuel Brandon's play, *The Tragicomoedi of the
vertuous Octavia*, 1598.

A QUEENLY ROSE OF SOUND
WITH TUNE FOR SCENT ...

Philip Bourke Marston (1850–87), English poet,
from "Sonnets to a Voice".

"Thy voice around me hover'd like a song
Of silver-tongued desire. Thy wondrous voice ...
Low, low and clear – a song of longing love;
Half sadness – half the soulful ecstasy
That, deeper far than mortal thought may fathom,
Stirs dimly thro' the hearts of men ... Thy lips
Have suck'd the sweetness of some magic draught –
And plead each echo of remote desire
That wanders o'er the earth. I hear the chant
Of winds in springtime waking northern lands;
The home-winds balmy welcome toward the sail;
The kiss of emerald ripples on the rims
Of dreaming isles ...
The sound of dim forests whispering of sleep –
That all, throughout thy voice's modulations,
Drift, as the drowsy undertones thro' melody
Wrought by the haunting witchery of harps."

Antony to Cleopatra
Vernon Nott (1878–?), Canadian writer,
from *Cleopatra with Antony, A Poetic Dialogue*, 1904.

Gustave Moreau,
Cléopâtre, *Louvre.*

39

"What, you be forgotten?

Nonsense, you do not realize how powerful longing can be,
Nor how implacable a secret that consumes.
One can live without bread within the walls of a besieged city,
One can live without fire in the snowy wastes,
One can live without water in the African deserts,
One can live without air in the mouth of the volcano,
But in this madness where the mind reels,
One could not live for one day without thinking of you!
For one day without remembering you,
  without calling you twenty times,
Without trying to hear the sweetness of your voice,
Without inhaling the pure air that you exhale ..."

A slave reassures Cleopatra that Antony cannot have forgotten her
from Delphine de Girardin's *Cléopâtre*, 1847.

"The world holds not the woman of whom I am afraid.
But I'm jealous of the rapture I tasted in his kiss,
And I would not that another should share with me that bliss.
No joy would I deny him, let him cull it where he will,
So mistress of his bosom is Cleopatra still;
So that he feels forever, when he Love's nectar sips,
'Twas sweeter, sweeter, sweeter when tasted on my lips ...
For I would scorn to hold him by but a single hair
Save his own longing for me when I'm no longer there;
And I will show you, Roman, that for one kiss from me
Wife, fame, and even honour to him shall nothing be!"

Mary Bayard Clark, 19th-century American poet, from "Cleopatra's Soliloquy".

Salvatore Fiume, Cleopatra and Antony.

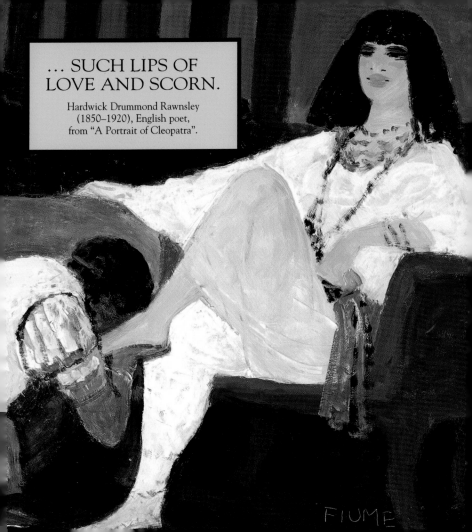

... SUCH LIPS OF
LOVE AND SCORN.

Hardwick Drummond Rawnsley
(1850–1920), English poet,
from "A Portrait of Cleopatra".

Crushing her vivid mouth, more crimson still
With the protesting blood, he drinks his fill
From the near fountain of her fragrant lips
And bites the rosebuds of her fingertips.

C. Edith Ironmonger, 20th-century English writer,
from *Cleopatra, A Narrative Poem*, 1924.

SUCH MOUTHS GET KISSED AND
KISS AGAIN, BUT ARE THOSE
THAT COUNT THE KISSES,
KEEP THEM IN A BOX FOR
FUTURE REFERENCE.

Mary Butts (1892–1937), British-born American author,
from *Scenes from the Life of Cleopatra*, 1935.

She shed her kisses here
and there like flower-petals.

E. Barrington,
from *The Laughing Queen*, 1929.

"I want to wear out your
lips with passionate kisses;
And to expire on your breast
In the ecstasy of love."

Antony and Cleopatra speaking in chorus
Marco D'Arienzo (1811–77), Italian writer,
from *Cleopatra*, 1875.

My lips held fast the
mouth o' the world …

Algernon Charles Swinburne,
from *The Masque of Queen Bersabe, a Miracle Play*.

"We have kissed away
Kingdoms and provinces."

Scarus to Enobarbus, Act III, 10 from William
Shakespeare's play, *Antony and Cleopatra*, 1607.
Shakespeare's play derives its history from
Plutarch. The first part of the play is notable for
its dark and erotic comedy. However, the
characters of Antony and Cleopatra emerge in
their full nobility as the tragedy draws to a close.

CLEOPATRA'S

"YOUR CLEOPATRA;
DOLABELLA'S CLEOPATRA;
EVERY MAN'S CLEOPATRA."

Ventidius to Antony, Act IV from John Dryden's play, *All For Love*, 1677.

Every man who approached her was regarded as her lover.

Oskar von Wertheimer, from *Cleopatra, A Royal Voluptuary*, 1931.

Cleopatra did not possess supreme beauty, she possessed
supreme seductiveness. As Victor Hugo said of a celebrated
theatrical character, "She is not pretty, she is worse."

Henry Houssaye, from *Cleopatra, A Study.*

LIBIDO

MODESTY WAS NOT A VIRTUE ON THE BANKS OF THE NILE.

Gaston Delayen, from *Cleopatra*, 1934.

Salvatore Fiume, Cleopatra and Cæsar.

"You know she's not much used to lonely nights."

Ventidius to Antony, Act IV from John Dryden's play, *All For Love*, 1677.

By whatever name we may describe Circe, Delilah, Heloise, Yseult, Carmen, the Sirens and the Valkyries, we may hold as certain that women whose presence throws men into a fever must always be great inspirers ... If Cleopatra pursued her glorious course on a higher level than her celebrated rivals it was because she possessed in a higher degree the sovereign gift of life which transforms the commonplace and creates an atmosphere of emotion.

Claude Ferval [Baronne Aimery Harty de Pierrebourg] (b. 1856 or 1858), French writer, from *The Life and Death of Cleopatra*.

Cleopatra's whole character is the triumph of the voluptuous, of the love of pleasure and the power of giving it, over every other consideration.

William Hazlitt (1778–1830), English writer, from "Characters of Shakespear's Plays: Antony and Cleopatra" in *The Complete Works*, 1817.

Cleopatra's palace, with its oriental setting, the languorous beauties of Cleopatra herself, the sinuous nakedness of her slaves, all has a certain serpentine and ungodly attraction – something of hot unchastity.

George Wilson Knight (1897–1985), English writer and critic, from *The Imperial Theme*, 1931.

Heart-consuming love, sensual pleasure, burning passion, youth inexhaustible and ever fresh, the promise of bliss to come, – she expressed all!

Théophile Gautier, from *Cleopatra*, 1845.

But Cleopatra's love ... is without any moral dignity.

Eduard Hülsmann, 19th-century German writer, from *Shakspeare: Sein Geist und seine Werke*, 1856.

"Hot, hot, and craving, as the gulph of hell, Is woman's appetite!"

Antony to Alexas, Act II, 7 from Henry Brooke's play, *Antony and Cleopatra*, 1778.
In this scene, Antony believes that Cleopatra has betrayed him with Ptolemy Artuasdes, her brother.

[Her] pleasures were as ocean-tides; they surged up from the dark depths of her impassioned soul.

Henry Giles (1809–82), American clergyman and lecturer,
from *Human Life in Shakespeare*, 1868.

... delitious dame,
(Thou royall concubine, and queene of lust).

Samuel Daniel (1562?–1619), English poet and historian,
from *A Letter from Octavia to Marcus Antonius*, 1599.
In her letter, Daniel's Octavia tries to expose the sordid machinery of Cleopatra's seductions to her erring husband, the Queen's victim. Samuel Daniel was a tutor in Mary Sidney's house. He wrote his first play, *The Tragedie of Cleopatra*, at the age of 32 as a companion piece to Sidney's *Mark Antony*, and five years later he wrote his damning *A Letter from Octavia to Antony*.

LECHEROUS CANOPUS'S PROSTITUTE QUEEN.

Propertius (c. 50–c. 15 BC), Roman poet.

Note: Romans thought sexual depravity a sign not of moral failure but of weakness. Cleopatra will always be associated with pearls, which symbolize female lustfulness. Lucy Hughes-Hallett, in her excellent book, *CLEOPATRA Histories, Dreams and Distortions*, records that "the Cleopatra Grip", a skill in contracting the vaginal muscles, is a technique known among professional courtesans even today. In his book *Pantagruel*, Rabelais depicts Cleopatra in hell as "a crier of onions" – a woman who sells onions in the street, proclaiming her wares in a loud voice. An onion is symbolic of a huge pearl, which itself symbolizes female lust.

I shall be Venus Genetrix and greet
With chaste lips this Dionysus I first saw at fourteen.
I shall trap his quintessent heart and waltz it round
My own Gods quivering in unmarked graves.
For so long as one dank breath escapes from Karnak,
So long as one brace of bones, churns like rolling dice,
Away from Delphi's oracle, so long as one
Handful of red earth crumbles under the
Saturnine & Equatorial sun of Ethiopia's Pharaohs
I refuse to be eclipsed by Cæsar's shadow & Cæsar's sex,
For, so long as Egypt rests its shaven head
On my Cleopatrian breasts,
Cæsar's manhood curled loosely in my hand,
Rome, don't cross me.

Barbara Chase-Riboud, from *Portrait of a Nude Woman as Cleopatra*, 1987.

CLEOPATRA
Night weighs down heavy on the darkened Nile.
Stars burn; pale Cleopatra kneels, and bares
her breast: her women, shocked, recoil; she tears
her tunic with a gesture grandly vile,

and on the lofty terrace flaunts, entire,
ripe as a love-blown fruit, her virgin form.
She shimmers, nude, uncoiling to the warm
devouring wind, a serpent of desire.

Dark flower of sex, that rides the breeze of night!
To pleasure her (the tawny eyes flash bright)
the world shall now her fleshly perfume take ...

The Sphynx becalmed on ocean monotone
feels under him the mighty desert wake,
and thrill of fire invade his silent stone.

Albert Samain (1858–1900), French poet, translated by Timothy Ades.

Laurence Alma-Tadema, Cleopatra, 1875, Art Gallery of New South Wales, Sydney.

There before me lay Cleopatra in all her beauty, which thrilled the beholder as he is thrilled by the rushing of the midnight gale.

Sir Henry Rider Haggard (1856–1925), English novelist,
from *Cleopatra, being an account of The Fall and Vengeance of Harmachis,
The Royal Egyptian, as set forth by his own hand*, 1889. It was on this decadent version of
the story that Fox Studios based their 1917 film starring the great vamp, Theda Bara.

Cleopatra's whole nature seemed to be shaken by a perpetual storm. She was all movement, her faculties were ever agog ... the contrast between her feminine softness and her wild fury, between her grace and her passion, must have constituted a charm but rarely met. In her presence boredom, whether by night or day, was out of the question.

Oskar von Wertheimer, from *Cleopatra, A Royal Voluptuary*, 1931.

The feisty queen, to whom everything is becoming – scolding, laughing, crying – at every instant another face, at each breath a passion, flesh struggling with a desire for more love, more life, more pleasure, at every moment, the queen with ten tongues; she spoke them all ... And she also made all the tongues of all the parts of the body speak, and she knew also all the songs of the blood.

Hélène Cixous and Catherine Clément, contemporary French writers, from *The Newly Born Woman*, 1986.

At every moment we are necessarily aware of the gross, the mean, the disorderly womanhood in Cleopatra, no less than of the witchery and wonder ... a spirit of *life* in Cleopatra, quick, shifting, multitudinous, incalculable, fascinates the eye, and would, if it could, lull the moral sense to sleep.

Edward Dowden (1843–1913), Irish Shakespearean scholar, critic and poet, from *Shakspere: A Critical Study of His Mind and Art*, 1875.

"Age cannot wither her, nor custom stale
Her infinite variety. Other women cloy
The appetites they feed, but she makes hungry
Where most she satisfies; for vilest things
Become themselves in her, that the holy priests
Bless her when she is riggish."

Enobarbus to Mæcenas and Agrippa, Act II, 2
from William Shakespeare's play, *Antony and Cleopatra*, 1607.

… such a woman, source of beauty, more than plenty –
running over. She overfills without saturating. Scarcely
has she satisfied before she gives another thing to desire
for which she invents another satisfaction.

Hélène Cixous and Catherine Clément, from *The Newly Born Woman*, 1986.

O wonderful inventory of inventiveness,
a happiness beyond comparison in
memory, of which, of all things,
Cleopatra was endowed.

Paganino Gaudenzio, from *Di Cleopatra Reina D'Egitto: la Vita Considerata*, 1642.

She became so debauched that she often sold herself as a prostitute; but she was so beautiful that many men bought a night with her at the price of their own death.

Aurelius Victor, 4th-century Roman historian and biographer, from *De Viris Illustribus*.

Who talks to me of reason now?
It would be more delight
To have died in Cleopatra's arms
Than be alive to-night.

Robert Louis Stevenson (1850–94), Scottish novelist and traveller,
from "After Reading 'Antony and Cleopatra'".

Often she abandoned herself to wild frenzies, and ofte

he put to death those who submitted to

Marco D'Arie

The Queen announces, lifting
Her brow again, with solemn gaze:
"Hear me! This day it is my pleasure
To make us equals in my sight.
To you my love were highest blessing;
But you may buy this bliss tonight.
Behold the marketplace of passion!
For sale I offer nights divine;
Who dares to barter in this fashion
His life against one night of mine? …
Receive ye this my pledge: unto the languid dawn
I promise to obey my rulers' utmost wishes
With wondrous tenderness, strange arts, the deep delicious
Cup ever newly filled with love's entrancing wine …
But when into my chamber through the curtains shine
Young Eos' early rays – I swear by your grim shade
Their heads shall fall that morn beneath the headsman's blade."

Claire Luce in Antony and Cleopatra, Stratford, 1945.

Alexander Pushkin (1799–1837), Russian poet, from "Kleopatra".
Pushkin had been influenced by the controversy surrounding Alexander Soumet's
1824 play, Cléopâtre, which cast the queen as a tragic heroine rather than as a wicked
hussy. Pushkin's poem, written in 1824 but published posthumously in Russian in
1838, revived the old tale against her: that she would spend a night with any man
provided that she could take his life the following morning. Pushkin, however, gives
the act an almost religious tone: Cleopatra sacrifices herself and her victim in a ritual
violation. This theme was explored again by Pushkin in "Egyptian Nights" in 1835, and
soon after by Théophile Gautier. The exotic Nile theme, at this time, had been made
fashionable by Napoleon's conquests in Egypt and subsequent archæological discoveries.

"I am fire and air."

Cleopatra to Iras and Charmian, Act V, 2 from William Shakespeare's play, *Antony and Cleopatra*, 1607.

"O what timid stuff chastity is!"

Cleopatra's comment Talbot Mundy (1879–1940), English novelist, from *Queen Cleopatra*, 1929.

"I take no pleasure In aught an eunuch has."

Cleopatra to her eunuch Mardian, Act I, 5 from William Shakespeare's play, *Antony and Cleopatra*, 1607.

"My vagabond desires no limits found, For lust is endless, pleasure hath no bound."

Cleopatra to Eras, Act II, I from Samuel Daniel's play, *The Tragedie of Cleopatra*, 1594.

CLEOPATR

Claude Rains and Vivien Leigh in Cæsar and Cleopatra, 1945.

SHE NATURALLY HAD A VERY SUBTLE, PIERCING WIT.

Dio Cassius, from *Roman History*.

A'S MIND

The beautiful and brilliant Cleopatra was her father's favourite ... She followed the history courses of Diodorus, the literary conferences of Didymus, the lessons on astronomy given by Sosigenes, and was also present at the gymnastic displays held in preparation for the Olympian games. The young princess completed her education and refined her taste by conversing with the scholars, poets, artists, and actors that were daily visitors at the court.

Désiré de Bernáth, early 20th-century Hungarian writer, from *Cleopatra: her Life and Reign*, 1901.

Oh, oh, oh, I have sat holding that cat-like bundle on my lap, drumming my fingers on ten brown toes and heard a soft voice from my shoulder asking me how to prevent banking houses from discouraging the industry of the people and what are the just wages of a chief of police relative to those of the governor of a city. Everyone in our world, my Lucius, everyone is lazy in mind except you, Cleopatra, this Catullus, and myself.

Julius Cæsar describes Cleopatra in a letter to his friend Lucius
Thornton Wilder (1897–1975), American writer, from *The Ides of March*, 1948.

I was ever more astonished at the wealth and splendour of her mind, that for richness and variety was as a woven cloth of gold throwing back all lights from its changing face.

Sir Henry Rider Haggard, from *Cleopatra, being an account of The Fall and Vengeance of Harmachis, The Royal Egyptian, as set forth by his own hand*, 1889.

Cleopatra from first to last was dominated by love of country and desire of power. The fear that Egypt might slip away from the Ptolemaic dynasty and become a province of Rome must have been her day-and-night obsession ... When all was said and done, Egypt was her real lover.

Philip Beaufoy Barry (b. 1878), English stage writer and popular historian, from *Sinners Down the Centuries*, 1929.

Even in her embraces Cleopatra did not forget the dictates of politics.

Oskar von Wertheimer,
from *Cleopatra, A Royal Voluptuary*, 1931.

*"I am more brain than body ...
I shiver in my own air sometimes."*

A young Cleopatra explains the coldness of her passion to Charmian
E. Barrington, from *The Laughing Queen*, 1929.

Drunk with destruction, dazed with dark delights, She dreamt herself a deity at Rome.

Horace (65–8 BC), Roman poet, from *Odes*.
Horace may well have known Cleopatra personally. He was in his twenties during her time in Rome. He damns Cleopatra for enslaving the noble Roman, Antony.

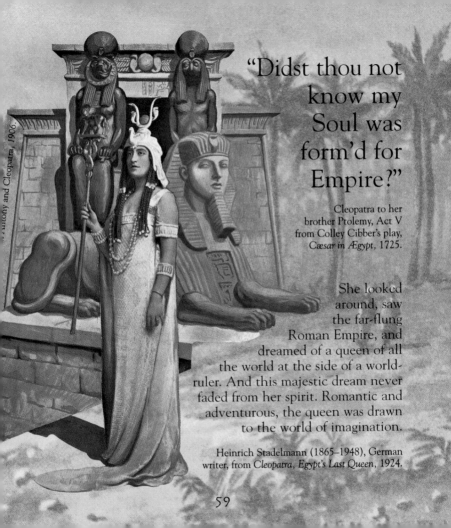

Antony and Cleopatra, 1906.

> "Didst thou not know my Soul was form'd for Empire?"

Cleopatra to her brother Ptolemy, Act V from Colley Cibber's play, *Cæsar in Ægypt*, 1725.

She looked around, saw the far-flung Roman Empire, and dreamed of a queen of all the world at the side of a world-ruler. And this majestic dream never faded from her spirit. Romantic and adventurous, the queen was drawn to the world of imagination.

Heinrich Stadelmann (1865–1948), German writer, from *Cleopatra, Egypt's Last Queen*, 1924.

CLEOPATRA'S
WILES

"I have learned love in Egypt. All I know
I have not taught even to Antony;
And I know all things."

A speech by Cleopatra
Arthur Symons (1865–1945), Welsh poet, from *Cleopatra*, 1916.

She possessed the key to the arcana of love. From the old secret books of the East she had learned, it was said, the virtues of the precious stones and the miraculous power of emeralds, sapphires, pearls, as determined by the Cabala. The Sanskrit teachings, although jealously guarded by the sacred dancing-girls, had revealed to her the erotic enchantment – compounded of intoxicating love-potions, subtle perfumes, artful caresses, opportune suggestions, curiosity ever unsatisfied, and wild transports – of the Kama Sutra, at once ideal and voluptuous, spiritual and luxurious, into which one was initiated on the altars of Astarte or in the temples of Siva.

Gaston Delayen, from *Cleopatra*, 1934.

Lavender lyddite [a high explosive] in a cut glass torpedo;
pink arsenic, violet-scented; a poignard in a peony ...

Fox Studios' description of Theda Bara's Cleopatra, 1916.

Hers was indeed the poetry of coquetry.

Charles Cowden Clarke (1787–1877), English critic and scholar,
from *Shakespeare–Characters, Chiefly Those Subordinate*.

Her charm is of the sense-intoxicating kind …

Georg Brandes (1842–1927), Danish writer, from *William Shakespeare A Critical Study*, 1898.

There is no resisting her nor escaping from her …

Henry Norman Hudson (1814–86), American writer,
from *Shakespeare: His Life, Art and Characters*, 1872.

He who has tasted her,
the unequalled one,
is forever hungry for her.

Hélène Cixous and Catherine Clément,
from *The Newly Born Woman*, 1986.

She has a serpent's grace, a serpent's attraction,
dangerous as Eve, serpent-beguiled.

George Wilson Knight, from *The Imperial Theme*, 1931.

"I go to her in spite of myself, as a bird goes to a snake."

Adolph Stahr (1805–76), German writer, from *Cleopatra*, 1864.

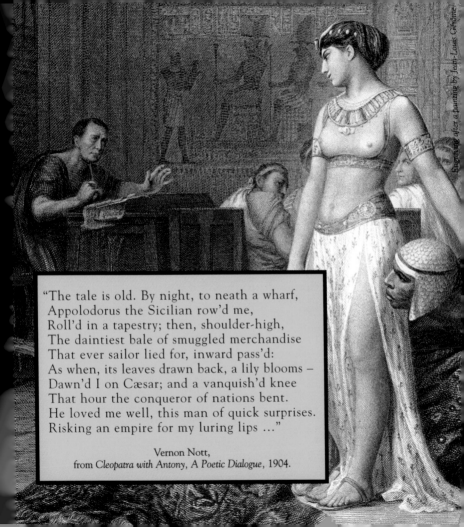

Engraving after a painting by Jean-Louis Gérôme

"The tale is old. By night, to neath a wharf,
Appolodorus the Sicilian row'd me,
Roll'd in a tapestry; then, shoulder-high,
The daintiest bale of smuggled merchandise
That ever sailor lied for, inward pass'd:
As when, its leaves drawn back, a lily blooms –
Dawn'd I on Cæsar; and a vanquish'd knee
That hour the conqueror of nations bent.
He loved me well, this man of quick surprises.
Risking an empire for my luring lips …"

Vernon Nott,
from *Cleopatra with Antony, A Poetic Dialogue,* 1904.

She was carried into the building by a servant and dumped down before the astonished Cæsar. It was done in a mood of passionate adoration, mystically mixed with a religious quasi-identification of Cæsar with Osiris, under-written by the indubitable fact that Cæsar was indeed the priest-king of the religion of the West ... he had never had a compliment like this before.

Oliver Coligny de Champfleur Ellis, (b. 1889), English writer, from *Cleopatra in the Tide of Time*, 1947.

Now we see him with the crown of her sex, with such a creature as he had never before even dreamed of; and the most beautiful of women stood in the presence of the most remarkable man of the century.

Adolph Stahr, from *Cleopatra*, 1864.

Thinking that she would obtain her kingdom if she could draw Cæsar, the conquerer of the world, into lustfulness, and being very beautiful and captivating anyone she desired with her shining eyes and her eloquence, with little trouble she brought the lustful prince to her embraces.

Giovanni Boccaccio (1313–75), Italian poet and humanist, from *De Cleopatra Regina Egiptio* in *De Claris Mulieribus*, 1374. Boccaccio saw Cleopatra as a metaphor for rapaciousness, sadism and cupidity.

Note: Cæsar, no doubt beguiled by Cleopatra, had other reasons to pass time with her in Alexandria. He needed cash to pay his army, and so to collect an old debt of 6,000 talents promised by Cleopatra's father, Ptolemy Auletes, as the price of Rome propping up his regime in Egypt. Cæsar mentions Cleopatra only once in his own writings. Writing in the third person, he explains in a single sentence how he restored Cleopatra to the joint throne of Egypt following her dispute with Ptolemy XIII. When Cleopatra followed him to Rome, she lived not with him but in a villa on the South bank of the Tiber. Cæsar never acknowledged Cæsarion as his son.

CÆSAR CONFIDES TO ANTONY

To be in love with her
Is to be in love
With all that time tells us
Of the mystery of wanting.
With all that time tells us
Of how we may laugh
And when we may touch
And what a man can know.
And the woman takes me
Like a queen, piercing pain
And destroying death.

Bruce Feld (b. 1942), American actor and writer,
from "Cæsar Confides to Antony" in *Cleopatra in the Night
and Other Poems.*

Cæsar and Pompey knew her when she was but a
young thing, and knew not then what the world
meant: but now she went to Antonius at the age
when a woman's beauty is at the prime, and she is
also of the best judgement. So, she furnished
herself with a world of gifts, store of gold and silver,
and of riches and other sumptuous ornaments …
But yet she carried nothing with her wherein she
trusted more than in herself …

Plutarch, from *Parallel Lives.*

"She came from Egypt.
Her galley down the silver Cydnos rowed ..."

Antony to Dolabella, Act III
from John Dryden's play, *All For Love*, 1677.

"The barge she sat in, like a burnished throne,
Burned on the water. The poop was beaten gold;
Purple the sails, and so perfumèd that
The winds were lovesick with them. The oars were silver,
Which to the tune of flutes kept stroke and made
The water which they beat to follow faster,
As amorous of their strokes. For her own person,
It beggared all description. She did lie
In her pavilion, cloth-of-gold of tissue,
O'erpicturing that Venus where we see
The fancy outwork nature. On each side her
Stood pretty dimpled boys, like smiling cupids,
With divers-coloured fans, whose wind did seem
To glow the delicate cheeks which they did cool ..."

Enobarbus to Agrippa, Act II, 2
from William Shakespeare's play, *Antony and Cleopatra*, 1607.*

It was her whim to show him on that night
All she was queen of; like a perfect dream,
Wherein there should be gathered in one sight
The gold of many lives ...

Arthur W. E. O'Shaughnessy (1844–81), English poet,
from "Cleopatra", 1870.

65

"On each side as he passed were placed beautiful Women ... every step he took, Beauties of a more exquisite Kind, and more richly dressed, attracted his Eyes. Thus I contrived to excite in his Mind an Idea of the Gradation of Beauty from the lowest to the highest Degree".

Cleopatra's seduction of Antony
Sarah Fielding (1710–68), English novelist,
from *The Lives of Cleopatra and Octavia*, 1757.

"I'll make thee drunken with my softest kiss!
I'll fill thy soul with pleasures so profound
That come what may, the memory of me
Will hold thy heart so long as life shall last."

Cleopatra to Antony, Act I
from Louis Payen's [Albert Liénard] libretto for the opera,
Cleopatra, by Jules Massenet, 1915.

"I serve him for his pleasure,
not his good; And thus I keep him."

Cleopatra tells Herod how she enthralls Antony
Arthur Symons, from *Cleopatra*, 1916.

"My Smiles were his Satisfaction, and my Frowns his Torment, this placed him quite in my Power."

How Cleopatra seduced Antony
Sarah Fielding, from *The Lives of Cleopatra and Octavia*, 1757.

Sid James and Amanda Bar

Well, I was presented. Mars, I suppose, to Venus.
And do you know she gave me the wickedest little
smile. Saw through it herself, bless her.

From Antony's letter to Lucius Torquatus Corbo
Mary Butts, from *Scenes from the Life of Cleopatra*, 1935.

But since mine eyes enricht their sight
With Cleopatra's face ...
My very thoughts fram'd all my wordes,
To Cleopatra's name ...
Mine eyes were blinde, mine eares were deaffe,
My minde did scencelesse prove:
But when they saw, heard, or perceiv'd.
Hir face, hir name, hir love ...
No pleasures could my fancie please.

Antony's letter to his despairing wife, Octavia
from Samuel Brandon's play, *The Tragicomoedi
of the vertuous Octavia*, 1598.

And yet I feel like holding a thanksgiving to all the women I ever loved who got me into training for this.

From Antony's letter to Lucius Torquatus Corbo
Mary Butts, from *Scenes from the Life of Cleopatra*, 1935.

n Carry on Cleo, 1964.

ANTONY

It is said that he was always very susceptible in this way, and that he had been enamoured of her long ago, when she was still a girl and he was serving as master of horse under Gabinius at Alexandria.

Straightaway Antony's interest in public affairs began to dwindle. Whatever Cleopatra ordered was done, regardless of laws, human or divine. While her sister Arsinoe was a suppliant in the temple of Artemis Leucophryne at Miletus, Antony sent assassins thither and put her to death ... So swiftly was Antony transformed, and this passion was the beginning and the end of evils that befell him.

Appian, 2nd-century Alexandrian historian,
from *The Roman History of Appian of Alexander*.

He allowed himself to be dragged along after the woman, as if he had become a part of her flesh and must go wherever she led him.

Plutarch, from *Parallel Lives*.

The majority of historians who have concerned themselves with these events assert that Cleopatra caught Antony in her net ... But, as a fact, it was Antony who desired Cleopatra, whatever the cost of her capture.

Désiré de Bernáth, from *Cleopatra: her Life and Reign*, 1901.

"ONE DAY PASSED BY, AND NOTHING SAW BUT LOVE;
ANOTHER CAME, AND STILL 'TWAS ONLY LOVE:
THE SUNS WERE WEARIED OUT WITH LOOKING ON,
AND I UNTIRED WITH LOVING.
I SAW YOU EVERY DAY, AND ALL THE DAY;
AND EVERY DAY WAS STILL BUT AS THE FIRST."

Antony to Cleopatra, Act II from John Dryden's play, *All For Love*, 1677.

Nervesa della Battaglia. Villa Berti, Veneto.

"Give me mine angle. We'll to th'river; there,
My music playing far off, I will betray
Tawny-finned fishes. My bended hook shall pierce
Their slimy jaws; and as I draw them up,
I'll think them every one an Antony,
And say 'Ah, ha! Y'are caught!'"

Cleopatra to Mardian and Charmian, Act II, 5
from William Shakespeare's play, *Antony and Cleopatra*, 1607.
At one of the fishing parties on the Nile, with which Cleopatra amused her lover,
Antony procured divers to put big fishes upon his hooks while under the water.
Cleopatra outwitted him, dispatching divers of her own. Antony's line brought up a
fried fish in place of a live one, to the vast entertainment of the queen.

CLEOPATRA'S

I imagine Cleopatra
very cosmopolitan.
She lived in Rome like
an American in Paris.

Anatole France

... Nor can I, without a pang, think back
on the arrogance of the queen herself when she
was living in her villa across the Tiber.

Cicero (106–43 BC), Roman orator, statesman and philosopher,
describing Cleopatra's time in Rome in a letter to his friend Atticus, June 13th, 44 BC.
Cicero disliked Antony and attacked him for his alleged venality, weakness for women, his lust
for slaughter, but most of all for being "un-Roman". Antony's passion for the Egyptian Queen
would fulfil all Cicero's early criticisms of his character. Cicero had no respect for Cleopatra herself, either. He regarded as mere gossip the news that Cleopatra had borne Cæsar's son, Cæsarion.
However, one must suspect that the great bibliophile Cicero was most offended by Cleopatra's
failure to send him the precious books she had promised him from her great library at Alexandria.

LUXURY

The whole World knows that *Cleopatra*
was the most magnificent Queen that ever lived.

Gautier de Costes de La Calprenède, from *Cleopatra*, 1658.

None could be more ingenious than Cleopatra in devising ways of
rioting through life, luxurious beyond description and full of subtlety.

Heinrich Stadelmann, from *Cleopatra, Egypt's Last Queen*, 1924.

She is considered as having carried the extravagance of sensual
luxury, and personal display and splendour, beyond the limits
that had ever before or have ever since been attained.

Jacob Abbott (1803–79), American clergyman and author,
from *History of Cleopatra, Queen of Egypt*, 1852.

Nothing was enough for this extravagant woman.
She was enslaved by her appetite so that the whole
world failed to satisfy the desires of her imagination.

Flavius Josephus (c. AD 27–100), Jewish historian and general,
from *The Antiquities of the Jews*.
Josephus was one of the fiercest of Cleopatra's critics, accusing her of trying to seduce
Herod of Judæa, and failing in the attempt.

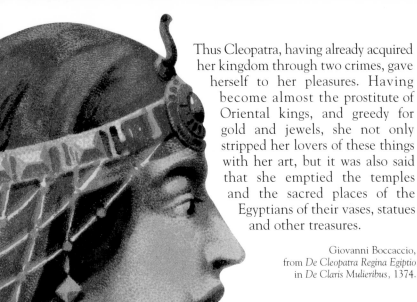

Thus Cleopatra, having already acquired her kingdom through two crimes, gave herself to her pleasures. Having become almost the prostitute of Oriental kings, and greedy for gold and jewels, she not only stripped her lovers of these things with her art, but it was also said that she emptied the temples and the sacred places of the Egyptians of their vases, statues and other treasures.

Giovanni Boccaccio,
from *De Cleopatra Regina Egiptio*
in *De Claris Mulieribus*, 1374.

The Egyptian woman demanded the Roman Empire from the drunken general as the price of her favours.

Lucius Annæus Florus (1st–2nd century AD),
African-born Roman historian and poet, from *Epitome of Roman History*.
Florus is rated more highly as a stylist than as an historian. He seems to be responsible for the earliest charge that Cleopatra attempted to seduce Octavian, and that she failed. In general, he saw her as a woman who sold her charms to nurture her enormous ambitions.

"I have breathed splendour

R. C. Woodville, from the Illustrated London News serialization of Henry Rider Haggard's Cleopatra, 1889.

"Jewels! jewels!

I love their every lovely name! …
Oh, that some god would sate my love of jewels!
To hoard the jewels of Tyre! … I'd heap them high
In softly-lighted rooms and visit them;
I'd love them, fondle them, plunging my arms
All shoulder-deep amid their mass'd delight;
I'd stand among them naked, and be robed
In showering hues no rainbow e'er hath dreamt!
And I would show the gaping world magnificence
Now unimagined …"

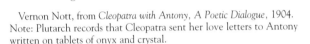

Vernon Nott, from *Cleopatra with Antony, A Poetic Dialogue*, 1904.
Note: Plutarch records that Cleopatra sent her love letters to Antony
written on tablets of onyx and crystal.

Having immoderately painted up her fatal beauty, neither content
with a sceptre her own, nor with her brother her husband,
covered with the spoils of the Red Sea, upon her neck and hair
Cleopatra wears treasures, and pants beneath her ornaments.

Lucan (AD 39–65), Roman poet, from *Pharsalia.*
Lucan's Cleopatra is modelled on the evil Messalina. He writes of the moment when
Cæsar arrives in Egypt, after defeating Pompey, but is lured from the path of conquest
by the fatal charms of Cleopatra. Lucan was put to death at the age of 25 by Nero. He
was writing a hundred years after Cleopatra died. Robert Graves has described him as
"the father of yellow journalism". In Lucan's eyes, Cleopatra's beauty was as dangerous
to Rome as Helen's had been to Troy.

as mean lives breathe breath."
James A. Mackereth, 20th-century English writer, from *The Death of Cleopatra, A DRAMATIC POEM*, 1920.

Cleopatra displayed her magnificence … Ivory clothed the entrance-hall; and Indian tortoise-shell, artificially coloured, was inlaid upon the doors, and its spots were adorned with many an emerald. Jewels glittered on the couches; the cups, tawny with jasper, loaded the tables, and sofas were bright with coverlets of diverse colours – most had long been steeped in Tyrian dye and took their hue from repeated soakings, while others were embroidered with bright gold and others blazed with scarlet … They served on gold a banquet of every dainty that earth or air, the sea or the Nile affords, all that extravagance, unspurred by hunger and maddened by idle love of display, has sought out over all the earth. Many birds and beasts were served that are divine in Egypt; crystal ewers supplied Nile water for their hands; the wine was poured into great jewelled goblets … They put on wreaths, twined of blooming nard and ever-flowering roses; they drenched their hair with cinnamon …

A description of the banquet Cleopatra prepared for her new lover Julius Cæsar, Lucan, from *Pharsalia*.

There were formerly two pearls, the largest that had been ever seen in the whole world: Cleopatra, the last of the queens of Egypt, was in possession of them both, they having come to her by descent from the kings of the East.

Pliny the Elder (AD 23–79), Roman scholar, from *The Natural History*.

It was a life of extravagance run mad. They did strange things ... Once, at a feast, Cleopatra wagered Antony that she would spend 10 million sesterces during the evening.

Philip Beaufoy Barry, from *Sinners Down the Centuries*, 1929.

... commanding them to bring a goblet of vinegar, the kind which, with its acidity, had the power to dissolve and liquify pearls, she grabbed one of the pearls from her ear and dropped it in the goblet. It dissolved instantly and she drank it down in one gulp. She wanted to do the same thing with the other, but was stopped by Plancus, who gave the judgement in favour of the queen. And so the pearl remained on her other ear thus preserved, and this one later came into the power of Augustus after the death of Cleopatra, and was divided into two parts, and put on the ears of the Venus in the temple of the Pantheon, for the enhancement of her glory.

Paganino Gaudenzio,
from *Di Cleopatra Reina D'Egitto: la Vita Considerata*, 1642.

laimed to wear a ring
Cleopatra herself. One of
ad himself delivered into
p in a carpet.

I would have loved to have been Cleopatra
in real life – providing I could choose
my own Antony.

Vivien Leigh (1913–67), British actress

The demands made upon the actress who is to play Cleopatra are infinitely greater [than those made on the actor playing Antony]. She has to suggest not only great beauty but the highest degree of personal fascination and magnetism that femininity has attained to on this planet ... I have forgotten to say that in addition to complete heartlessness she must have a heart of gold tucked about her somewhere, or at any rate something of that quality which made Lady Macbeth stick to her husband. In other words, she is to combine the qualities of great queen and unparalleled courtesan, together with the trifling accomplishment of being able to speak some of the greatest verse that Shakespeare ever wrote. No actress in my time has come within measurable distance of all this, excepting Janet Achurch, who made a very good shot at running the gamut of grandeur, pettiness, scorn, rage, jealousy, meanness, courage, cunning, and pure cattiness.

John O'London Weekly, September 29th, 1934,
reviewing the Old Vic production starring Mary Newcombe.

Plutarch's Cleopatra was already an assemblage of all that is fatal in womanhood ... Shakespeare ... makes the whole tingle with vitality and throb with beauty.

Charles Harold Herford (1853–1931), English writer,
writing about Antony and Cleopatra in The Eversley Shakespeare, 1899.

[Shakespeare] paints her as if the gypsy herself had cast her spell over him.

Thomas Campbell (1777–1844), Scottish poet,
from *Remarks on the Life and Writings of William Shakespeare*, 1838.

… That in her, the dark woman of Shakspere's Sonnets,
his own fickle, serpent-like, attractive mistress, is to
some extent embodied, I do not doubt.

Frederick James Furnivall (1825–1910), English philologist,
from the introduction to *The Leopold Shakespeare*, 1877.

Shakespeare's Cleopatra produces exactly the same effect on us that
is recorded of the real Cleopatra … We are conscious of a kind of
fascination against which our moral sense rebels, but from which
there is no escape.

Anna Jameson (1794–1860), Irish writer,
from *Characteristics of Women, Moral, Poetical, and Historical, Shakespeare's Heroines*, 1832.

No, if I should play the part as it should be played,
I should ever after hate myself.

The English actress Mrs Siddons, refusing to play Shakespeare's Cleopatra.
She did, however, take on the role in Dryden's play, *All for Love*.

Janet Achurch in Antony and Cleopatra, Olympic, 1897.

Sarah Bernhardt played Cleopatra on the London stage in 1879, a version by her intimate friend Victorien Sardou. It was a role she relished: exotic costumes, hysteria and death all featured. She was very fond of her asps – keeping two live garter snakes in a jewel box on her dressing table. During intervals, she often wrapped them round her wrists as bracelets. For the role, Bernhardt painted her hands red. Her friend, the English actress, Mrs Patrick Campbell, asked her why. Sarah's reply: "If I catch sight of my hand, it will be the hand of Cleopatra."

On stage, she never forgot for one moment that she was Cleopatra: she stormed, raved, wrecked the scenery and smashed goblets. A middle-aged British matron was heard to remark to her neighbour: "How different, how very different from the home life of our own dear Queen!"

On Armistice Day, 1937, I received the worst critical lambasting I ever experienced … John Mason Brown, later to caress me with superlatives, mowed me down: "Tallulah Bankhead barged down the Nile last night as Cleopatra and sank."

Tallulah Bankhead (1903–68), American actress, from *Tallulah, My Autobiography*, 1952.

Sarah Bernhardt in Cleopatra at London's Gaiety Theatre, 1879.

THERE HAVE BEEN MANY FILMS OF THE CLEOPATRA STORY, MOST OF THEM IMMENSELY COSTLY AND ACCIDENT-PRONE.

Hugo Vickers, contemporary British writer,
from *Vivien Leigh*, 1988.

Hugo Vickers was referring to the 1944 production of *Cæsar and Cleopatra*, filmed in Egypt, not only in appalling weather but with the additional problem that the local extras found that their shields, polished with fish-paste varnish, were not only edible but palatable. Vivien Leigh, the star, suffered a miscarriage during the filming and production was held up for six weeks.

More than 25 films and many television dramas were made of Cleopatra during the 20th century. The extravagance of the productions, particularly in films, came to be part of the Cleopatra legend. Fox Studios boasted that their 1917 film used 5,000 actors and 2,000 horses. Cecil B. de Mille's 1934 version was heralded for the unprecedented luxury of its sets. Gabriel Pascal's 1945 film of *Cæsar and Cleopatra* cost twice as much as *Gone with the Wind*. Twentieth Century-Fox's budget for the Elizabeth Taylor Cleopatra started at $2 million and finished at over $35 million. Like Elizabeth Taylor, Vivien Leigh enacted in real life the Other Woman role of Cleopatra. She and Laurence Olivier became lovers in 1936, when both were married to other people. They starred together in the Shakespeare and Shaw plays on the London and New York stages in 1951. Elizabeth Taylor's romance with Richard Burton blossomed while they were playing Cleopatra and Antony in the 1968 film. (Unfortunately it has not been possible to use pictures or text about Elizabeth Taylor in this book.)

... as Shakespeare's Cleopatra she speaks low notes of ... diamond-pointed beauty.

The *Evening Standard*, May 18th, 1951, reviewing the productions of Shakespeare's play, *Antony and Cleopatra* and Shaw's play, *Cæsar and Cleopatra*, performed on alternate nights by Vivien Leigh and Laurence Olivier at the St James Theatre, London. They later took the production to New York.

ISABELLA GLYN, 1849

Her death was sublime. With a magnificent smile of triumph, she is, as it were, translated to the shades, there to meet her imperial lover. Altogether Miss Glyn's performance of Cleopatra is the most superb thing ever witnessed on the modern stage.

Illustrated London News, October 27th, 1849, reviewing Isabella Glyn's memorable portrayal at Sadler's Wells in London.

THEDA BARA, 1917

She was divinely, hysterically, insanely malevolent.

Bette Davis (1908–89), American actress, speaking about Theda Bara. Fox invented a past for Bara in which she was born in the shade of the pyramids and nourished with crocodile milk. In fact, she came from the American Mid-West and was happily married.

I began thinking about the stir at the Museum when she came and wanted you to design her costume for this very movie. It's really a pity you didn't. It wouldn't have taken up any of your time for all she wears is a pair of sandals – one in one scene and the other in the next.

Herbert Winlock, assistant curator in the Department of Egyptian Art of the Metropolitan Museum of Art, New York, in a letter dated February 10th, 1918 to Albert Lythgoe, head of the same Department.

DOROTHY GREEN, 1930

Miss Dorothy Green, looking like one of the lovelier Lelys, gave a straight-laced and highly refrigerative performance of the arch-hussy.

James Agate in *The Sunday Times*, reviewing Dorothy Green's performance in the 1930 Old Vic production of Shakespeare's play, *Antony and Cleopatra*.

CLAUDETTE COLBERT, 1934

In his memoirs, Cecil B. de Mille, who directed her, recalled that Claudette Colbert was notoriously squeamish about small reptiles and almost pulled out of the film when she heard a snake was involved. On the day of shooting the snake scene, de Mille conquered her fears in a very creative way: he borrowed from the zoo the largest snake he could find, and approached her on the set. Colbert pleaded with him in terror to take it away. He then produced a small snake from his pocket which she happily accepted. He is alleged to have offered her the role with the words: "How would you like to be the wickedest woman in history?" It was said that when Colbert first kissed her Antony, three staff on the set fainted.

EDITH EVANS, 1947

By stressing the sheer trollop in *Cleopatra* at the expense of what Coleridge rather prettily called the criminality of her passion, Miss Edith Evans has legend on her side, and how brilliantly she does it!

Punch, January 8th, 1947, reviewing Edith Evans' performance in Shakespeare's play, *Antony and Cleopatra* at the Piccadilly Theatre, London.

PEGGY ASHCROFT, 1953

Peggy Ashcroft brought her astonishing Cleopatra to London last night. Critics squealed with alarm when they first saw it in Stratford six months ago. No wonder ... she does not just feed Antony on love. She feasts him till he is scared.

John Barber in the *Daily Express,* November 5th, 1953, reviewing Peggy Ashcroft's performance in Shakespeare's play, *Antony and Cleopatra* at the Prince's Theatre, London.

CLEOPATRA'S

This battle at Actium was both famous and great. From the fifth to the seventh hour, it raged with terrific losses on both sides and with the issue still undecided ... Queen Cleopatra was the first to flee with sixty of her swift vessels. Antony then pulled down the standard of the commander's ship and followed his wife in flight.

Paulus Orosius, 5th-century Spanish priest and chronicler,
from *Seven Books of History against the Pagans, The Apology of Paulus Orosius*.
He descibes how the sea battle between Octavian's and Antony's forces is lost because of the inconsistency of Cleopatra.

Driven now, she flies, through horrid ranks of death.
Pale upon wind and wave, she dreads her own:
And Father Nile, gigantic and distressed,
Draws home his vanquished child to sheltered streams,
The azure peace of his protective shades,
Spread abroad his fluid robes of rest.

A description of Cleopatra's flight from the Battle of Actium
Virgil (70–19 BC), Roman poet, from the *Æneid*.
It is thought that Virgil began the *Æneid* not long after Cleopatra died. The poem gave Rome its originary epic, and provided an eloquent mouthpiece for the values of Octavian's reign. The part concerning Cleopatra and Antony, in book VIII, is shown as a scene depicted on the shield borne by Æneas.

"My face too lovely caus'd my wretched case.
My face hath so entrap'd, so cast us downe."

Cleopatra, Act II from Robert Garnier's play, *Marc Antoine*, 1578.

FATAL

In the time that remained to them [after Actium and before Octavian's troops arrived], Antony and Cleopatra, seized with a sort of furious despair, gave themselves entirely to their old revels. A new Club was formed. No longer did people speak of the "Inimitables" – they spoke of "The Die-Togethers".

Philip Beaufoy Barry, from *Sinners Down the Centuries*, 1929.

Antonius was the first to seize the sword of a suicide; the queen, casting herself at Cæsar's feet, tried to attract his glances, but in vain, for her beauty was unable to prevail over his self-control. Her efforts were aimed not at saving her life, which was freely offered to her, but at obtaining a portion of her kingdom. Despairing of winning this from Cæsar and perceiving that she was being reserved to figure in his triumph, profiting by the carelessness of her guard, she betook herself to the Mausoleum …

Lucius Annæus Florus, from *Epitome of Roman History*.

BEAUTY

She put on her most beautiful apparel,
arranged her body in most seemly fashion,
took in her hands all the emblems of royalty...

Dio Cassius, from *Roman History*.

"You've heard of lovely Cleopatra
You know her history!
All men were victim to her lust
And yet she died in agony
And passed away and fell to dust."

Ginny Jenny's song, Act III, 1 from
Bertold Brecht's play, *The Threepenny Opera*, 1928.

Chelsea vase, © *The British Museum*

"Come Aspe, possesse thy mansion; freely feed
On these two hils, upon whose snowy tops
The winged *Cupid* oft has taken stand …"

Cleopatra's suicide speech over the dead body of Antony, Act V
from Thomas May's play, *The Tragedie of Cleopatra Queen of Egypt*, 1639.

Even with the asp at her breast,
She gave as a mother her breast to a mortal baby,
For a long immortal kiss.

Stephen Phillips (1864–1915), English poet and playwright,
from "A Woman to Shakespeare".

Note: It is hard to find a painting of Cleopatra that does not include the snake. It is probable that the snake used by Cleopatra was a species of cobra, a uræus, similar to the type sacred to Isis, the goddess with whom Cleopatra always identified herself. Although he was robbed of a live Cleopatra to display in chains at his triumph, Octavian ensured that an effigy of her was carried through the streets of Rome. According to Plutarch, a snake was shown clinging to the figure.

Later, the fatal reptile came to be endowed with many layers of symbolic meaning. In the Christian interpretation, Cleopatra's snake is like Eve's: the accessory of temptation. The snake belongs to Medusa, murderess of men. Cleopatra acquired the title "Serpent of the Nile". Of course, the snake is also a phallic symbol. When she takes the beast to her breast, Cleopatra is ravished by death – she makes death make love to her, just as she has seduced Cæsar and Antony. The sexual connotations of the act are inescapable in many paintings of her death, which persist in showing Cleopatra naked, even though it is fairly well documented that she dressed in the robes of Isis for her death.

A robot asp was made for the production of Marmontel's tragedy. It crawled and hissed most realistically, to the great delight of the Parisian audiences.

"I have

"When crowns were on my brow,
And nations did my rising greet,
And Cæsar grovelled at my feet,
I lived not – never lived till now."

Henry William Herbert (1807–58),
American poet, from "Cleopatra".

Immortal longings in me."

Cleopatra to Iras and Charmian, Act V, 2 from William Shakespeare's play, *Antony and Cleopatra*, 1607.

Silence embalms the shores of all the seas,
And Nile lies quiet to the leaning moon,
Lone-musing 'mong her deserts: canst not thou
Dream, heart, 'mong thine?
    Queens in old time have loved,
And lost their loves,
    and smiled on crumbling thrones
Beneath the bright indifference of the stars.
Great beauties reigned in Memphis' palaces
And gave love-ardent lips to mummied kings.
To all an end. The proudest dynasties
Shrink at the patience of a pyramid.
I am very weary. Ghostly Charmian,
Did we not die in dim years long ago?
This dust hath lengthy dreams.
    Where are the dancers?
I read that muteness in thy conscious face:
Gone, like sly vermin that scent death. Sing, girl;
Make soothing sounds: my senses bleed in me.

James A. Mackereth,
from *The Death of Cleopatra*, A DRAMATIC POEM, 1920.

"O see this face, the wonder of her life,
Retains in death, a grace, that graces death ...
And in this cheer th'impression of a smile,
Doth seem to show she scorns both death
    & Cæsar,
As glories that she could them so beguile,
And here tells death, how well
    her death doth please her."

Charmian, Act V, 2
from Samuel Daniel's play, *The Tragedie of Cleopatra*, 1594.

"SHE DIES FOR LOVE; BUT SHE HAS KNOWN ITS JOYS."

Alexas, Act III
from John Dryden's play, *All For Love*, 1677.

"Never did sleep
More slumberous, more infant-like, give forth
Its delicate breathings. You might see the hair
Wave, in stray ringlets, as the downy breath
Lapsed through the parted lips; and dream the leaf,
Torn from the rose and laid upon her mouth,
Was wafted by that zephyr of the soul ..."

Dolabella to Octavian
William Gilmore Simms (1806–70), American novelist and poet,
from "The Death of Cleopatra", 1853.

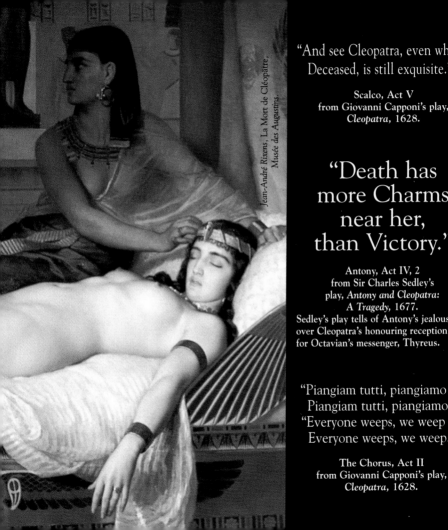

Jean-André Rixens, *La Mort de Cléopâtre*, Musée des Augustins

"And see Cleopatra, even when Deceased, is still exquisite."

Scalco, Act V
from Giovanni Capponi's play,
Cleopatra, 1628.

"Death has more Charms near her, than Victory."

Antony, Act IV, 2
from Sir Charles Sedley's
play, *Antony and Cleopatra:
A Tragedy*, 1677.
Sedley's play tells of Antony's jealousy
over Cleopatra's honouring reception
for Octavian's messenger, Thyreus.

"Piangiam tutti, piangiamo …
Piangiam tutti, piangiamo."
"Everyone weeps, we weep …
Everyone weeps, we weep."

The Chorus, Act II
from Giovanni Capponi's play,
Cleopatra, 1628.

The following sources are central to any study of Cleopatra, including this one: Geoffrey Bullough (ed), Narrative and Dramatic Sources of Shakespeare, Vol V, The Roman Plays, London, 1964 and Lucy Hughes-Hallett, CLEOPATRA Histories, Dreams and Distortions, Bloomsbury, 1990.

ACKNOWLEDGEMENTS

Every effort has been made to trace the copyright-holders of the material included in this book. In the event of any unwilling or inadvertent use of uncleared material, or for omitting the correct notification, the editor apologizes, and would be grateful to hear from the copyright-holder, and undertakes to amend any subsequent edition accordingly. The editors gratefully acknowledge permission of the following sources to use copyrighted material in this book:

TEXTUAL

The Common Liar, an essay on *Antony and Cleopatra* by Janet Adelman, published by Yale University Press, New Haven and London. Copyright © 1973 Yale University Press; *Alexander Pushkin: Collected Narrative and Lyrical Poetry* by Walter Arndt, published by Ardis Publishers in 1984; *Tallulah, My Autobiography* by Tallulah Bankhead, published by Victor Gollancz, reprinted by permission of Laurence Pollinger Limited. Copyright © 1952 Tallulah Bankhead; *The Threepenny Opera* by Bertolt Brecht, translated by Desmond Vesey and Eric Bentley, from *From the Modern Repertorie Series One*, edited by Eric Bentley, published by Indiana University Press. Copyright © 1949 Eric Bentley; *Scenes from the Life of Cleopatra* by Mary Butts, published by William Heinemann, reprinted by permission of Carcanet Press Limited. Copyright © 1935 Mary Butts; *Portrait of a Nude Woman as Cleopatra* by Barbara Chase-Riboud, published by Quill, William Morrow, New York in 1987, reprinted by permission of International Creative Management. Copyright © 1987 Barbara Chase-Riboud; *The Newly Born Woman* by Hélène Cixous and Catherine Clément, translated by Betsey Wing, published by I. B. Tauris & Co. Limited, London. Copyright © 1986 University of Minnesota; *Cleopatra in the Tide of Time* by Oliver Coligny de Champfleur Ellis, published by Williams and Norgate Limited in 1947, reprinted by permission of A & C Black (Publishers) Limited; "Cæsar Confides to Antony" from *Cleopatra in the Night and Other Poems* by Bruce Feld, published by Fithian Press. Copyright © 1999 Bruce Feld; *The Search for Cleopatra* by Michael Foss, published by Michael O'Mara Books. Copyright © 1997 Michael Foss; *Sesso e potere* by Enzo Gualazzi, published by Giorgio Mondadori, reprinted by permission of the author. Copyright © 1992 Enzo Gualazzi; *De Cleopatra Regina Egiptio*, from *De Claris Mulieribus* by Giovanni Boccaccio, translated by Guido A. Guarino, published by George Allen & Unwin in 1964, reprinted by permission of John Johnson (Authors' Agent) Limited. Copyright © 1963 Rutgers, The State University; *Signs of Cleopatra, History, Politics, Representation* by Mary Hamer, published in 1993 by Routledge, London and New York, reprinted by permission of the author. Copyright © 1993 Mary Hamer; *The Imperial Theme* by George Wilson Knight, published by Oxford University Press in 1931; "Cleopatra" by Albert Samain, translated by Tim Ades. Translation Copyright © 2001 Tim Ades; Sir Laurence Olivier's introduction to *Antony and Cleopatra* by William Shakespeare, published by the Folio Society in 1952; *Caesar and Cleopatra* by Bernard Shaw, reprinted by permission of the Society of Authors, on behalf of the Bernard Shaw Estate; *Cleopatra, Egypt's Last Queen* by Heinrich Stadelmann, translated from the German by Margaret M. Green, published by Routledge in 1931; *Cleopatra* from *Tragedies* by Arthur Symons, published by Heinemann in 1916; *The Romance of a Nose* by Gerald Tyrwhitt, published by Constable & Company Limited in 1941; *Vivien Leigh* by Hugo Vickers, published by Hamish Hamilton, reprinted by permission of Gillon Aitken Associates Limited. Copyright © 1988 Hugo Vickers; *Cleopatra, A Royal Voluptuary* by Oskar von Wertheimer, translated from the German by Huntley Patterson, published by Harrap in 1931; *The Ides of March* by Thornton Wilder reprinted by arrangement with The Wilder Family LLC and The Barbara Hogenson Agency. Copyright © 1945, 1973 by Thornton Wilder.

ILLUSTRATIVE

Front cover Vivien Leigh in *Cæsar and Cleopatra*, St James Theatre, 1951: photo by Angus McBean; page 82 Isabella Glyn in *Antony and Cleopatra*, Sadler's Wells, 1849; page 5 Lilly Langtry in *Antony and Cleopatra*, Princess Theatre, 1890; page 83 Edith Evans in *Antony and Cleopatra*, Old Vic, 1925; page 82 Dorothy Green in *Antony and Cleopatra*, Stratford, 1924: photo by Peter North; page 80 Sarah Bernhardt in *Cleopatra*, 1879; pages 78–79 Janet Achurch, *Antony and Cleopatra*, Olympic, 1897; page 83 Peggy Ashcroft in *Antony and Cleopatra*, Stratford, 1953: photo by Angus McBean; page 55 Claire Luce in *Antony and Cleopatra*, Stratford, 1945: photo by Angus McBean, all courtesy of the Raymond Mander & Joe Mitchenson Theatre Collection; page 70 illustration by Al Frueh of Lilli Palmer in the New York National Theatre's 1949 production of *Cæsar and Cleopatra*, reprinted by permission of the New Yorker Magazine, Inc; pages 34–35, 41 and 45 various pictures of Cleopatra by Salvatore Fiume, courtesy of Luciano Fiume, first published in Enzo Gualazzi, *Cleopatra, Sesso e Potere*, Giorgio Mondadori, Milano, 1992; page 69 Nervesa della Battaglia, school of Tiepolo, Cleopatra fresco at the Villa Berti. Copyright © Osvaldo Böhm, Venezia; pages 12–13 attributed to Michelangelo, 1887-5-2-120; pages 30–31 silver coin showing Cleopatra, BMC Ascalon 20; page 32 bust, possibly of Cleopatra SC.1873; page 44 terracotta Roman oil lamp Q900; page 86 Chelsea vase, Cleopatra Dying POT. CAT. II 28; page 87 Guercino, sepia drawing of Cleopatra 1895-9-15-709, all Copyright © The British Museum; page 17 *The Deaths of Antony and Cleopatra*, ROY.14.E.V f.339; page 29 anonymous encaustic portrait supposedly found in the ruins of the villa of the Emperor Hadrian at Tivoli, Rome. The illustration is the frontispiece from a published account by Emmanuele Berni, entitled *Peinture Grecque Ancienne, L'encaustique sur ardoise, représentant la Reine, Cléopâtre*, 1889, both by permission of The British Library; page 92 Cleopatra mask, courtesy of Mamelok Press Limited, Bury St Edmunds, England; pages 90–91 Jean-André Rixens, *La Mort de Cléopâtre*, courtesy of Musée des Augustins, Toulouse @ B. Delorme; pages 11 and 52–53 A. Cabanel, *Cléopâtre essayant des poisons sur des condamnés à mort*, courtesy of Koninklijk Museum Voor Schone Kunsten, Antwerp; page 27 Yasuhiro Tanigawa, *Cleopatra VII*, courtesy of the artist, with thanks to Mr Tadeo Hashimoto of Netcentury Inc. and Mr Akihiko Hatanaka of Shinseido Art Gallery; pages 7, 76 and 82 photographs of Theda Bara in *Cleopatra*, directed by J. Gordon Edwards, Copyright © 1917 Fox Film Corporation; pages 42–43 and 83 Claudette Colbert as Cleopatra, in the 1934 film of the same name, directed by Cecil B. de Mille. Copyright © 2000 by Universal City Studios, Inc. Courtesy of Universal Studios Publishing Rights. All Rights Reserved; pages 23, 56 and 77 photographs/kodachromes by Wilfred Newton of Vivien Leigh in the 1945 film of Bernard Shaw's *Cæsar and Cleopatra*, courtesy of Carlton International Media Ltd; pages 66–67 Amanda Barrie and Sid James in *Carry on Cleo*, directed by Gerald Thomas. Copyright © 1965 Anglo Amalgamated Productions, with thanks to Studio Canal+; pages 9 and 19 sculpture of Cleopatra 39.36, courtesy of The State Hermitage Museum, Saint Petersburg; page 15 sculpture of Cleopatra RC 1582, courtesy of The Rosicrucian Egyptian Museum, San José, California; page 24 Head of a Queen, Ptolemaic Period, 71.12, courtesy of The Brooklyn Museum of Art, New York, Charles Edwin Wilbour Fund; pages 36–37 Sculpture of Cleopatra-inv.38511, courtesy of Monumenti Musei e Gallerie Pontificie, The Vatican: photo: Vatican Museums; pages 38–39 Gustave Moreau, *Cléopâtre*, Louvre, Paris. Copyright © Photo RMN–J. G. Berizzi; page 49 Lawrence Alma-Tadema, *Cleopatra*, 1875, Art Gallery of New South Wales, Sydney; pages 3 and 88 Bust of Cleopatra 1976, Antikenmuseum Staatliche Museen zu Berlin, photographed by Johannes Laurentius. Copyright © Bpk 2000; page 14 Cleopatra relief at Denderah, Egypt, courtesy of Robert Partridge: The Ancient Egypt Picture Library; pages 33 and 59 Constance Collier in the 1906 Tree production of *Antony and Cleopatra*, from the *Play Pictorial*, No 54, vol IX; pages 64–65 Lawrence Alma-Tadema, *Antony and Cleopatra*, courtesy of Sotheby's Picture Library, London. All other items from the editor's own collection.

With thanks to Sally-Ann Ashton, Susan Walker, Peter Higgs and Hilary Williams at The British Museum, Richard Mangan, Lynne Curran, David Swift, Muriel Dahan, Karin Ter Glane and Phillip Ormond for their help.